What Goes Together?

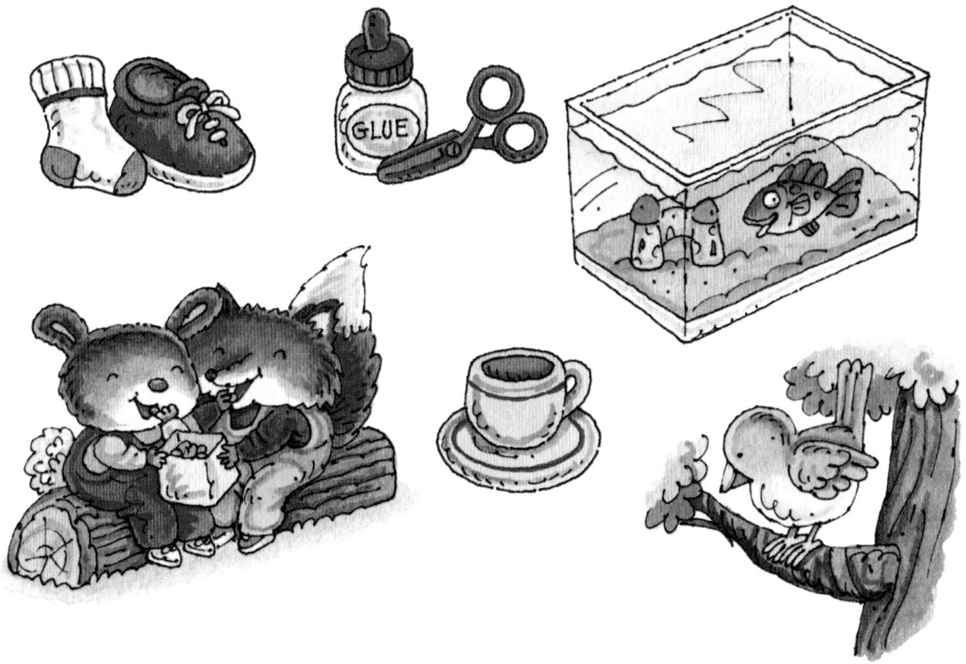

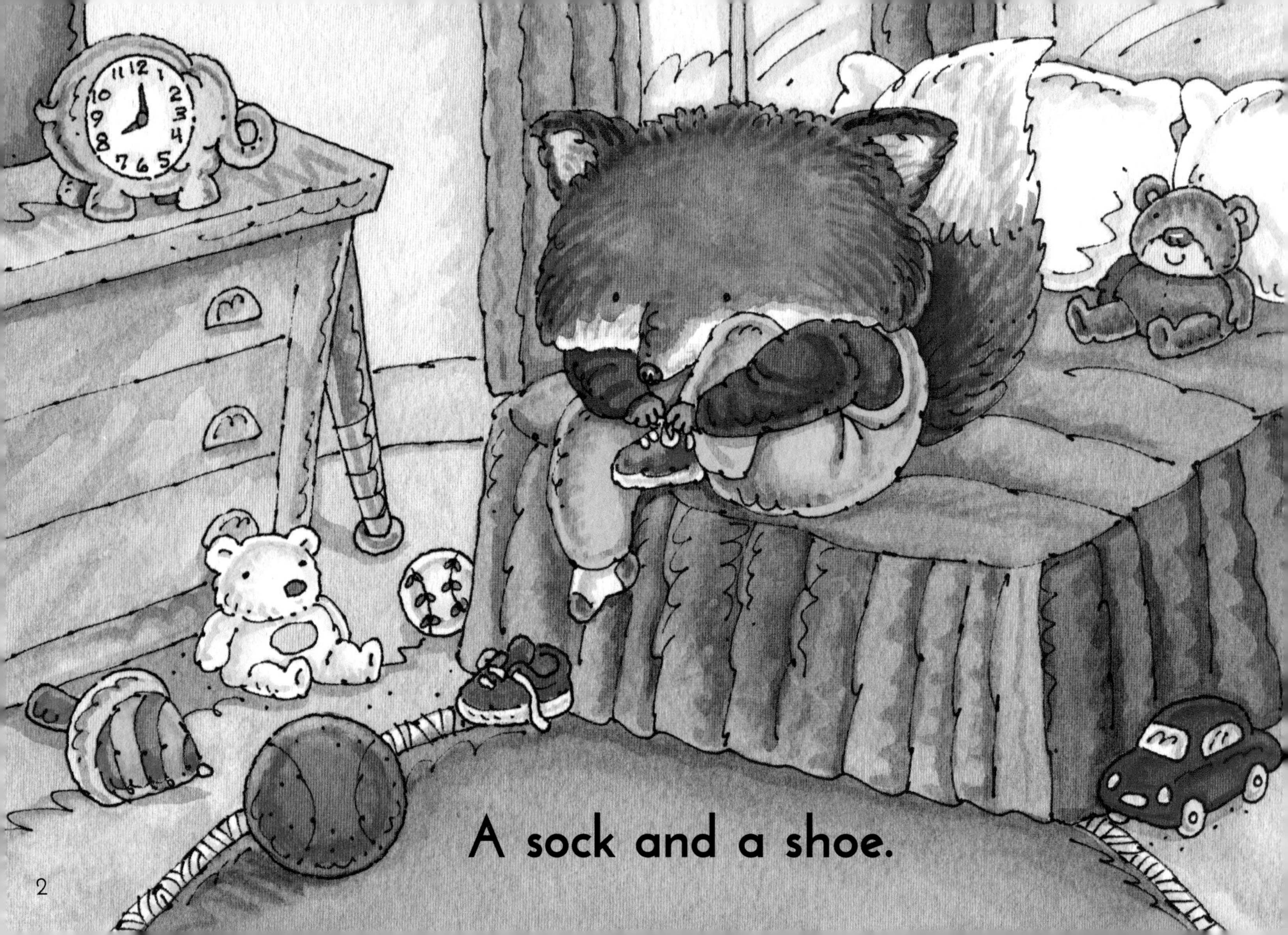

A sock and a shoe.

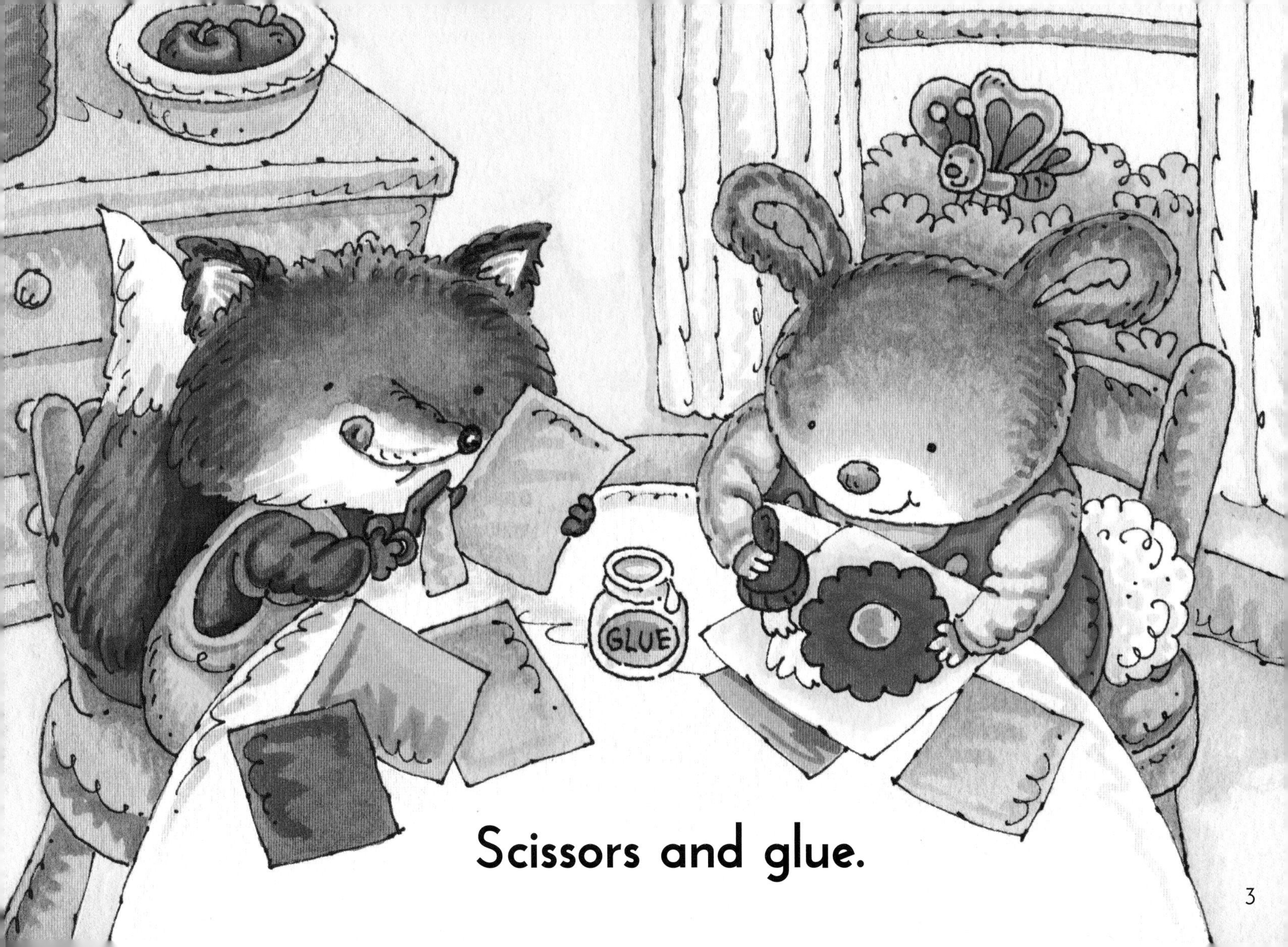

Scissors and glue.

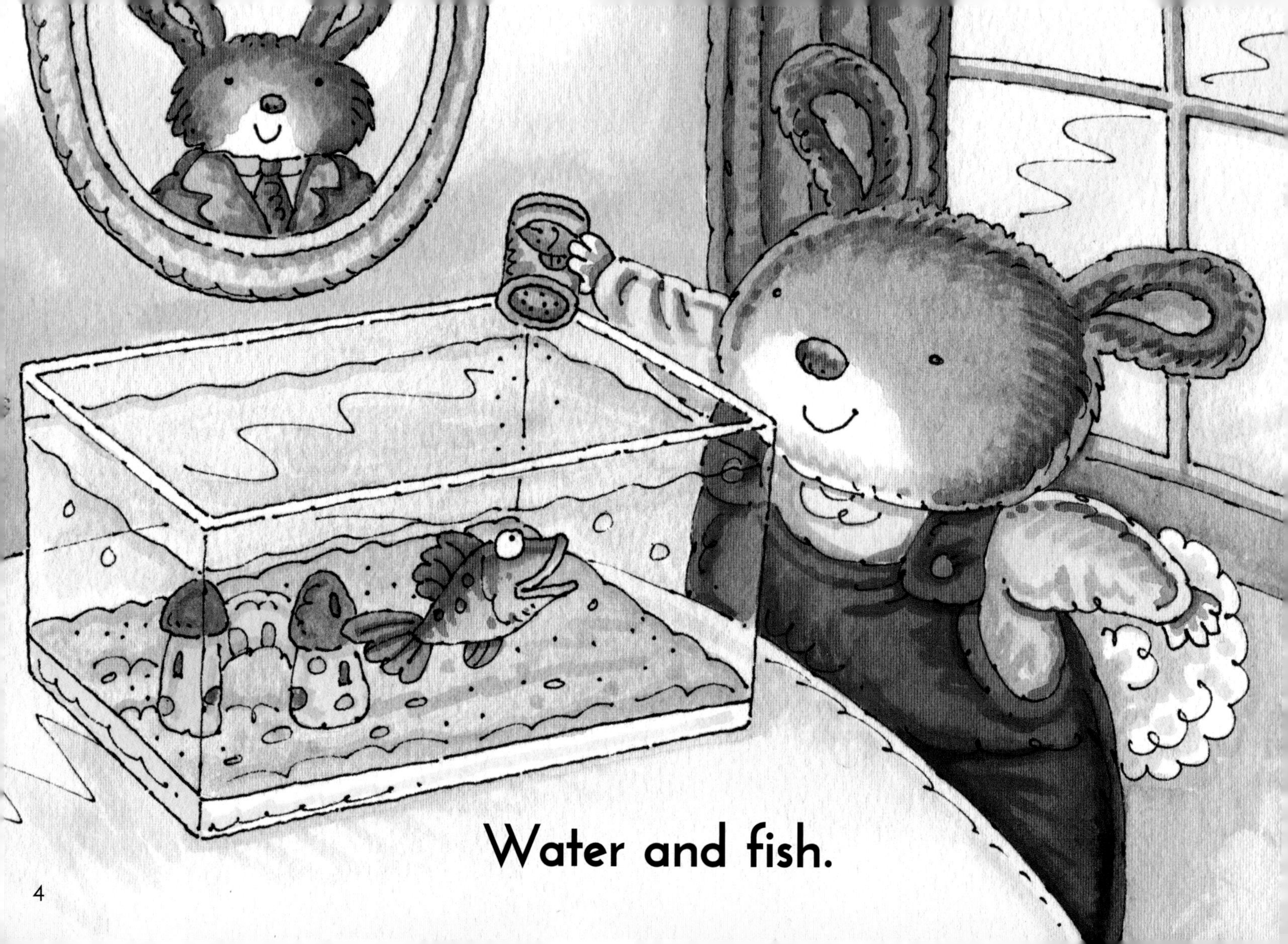

Water and fish.

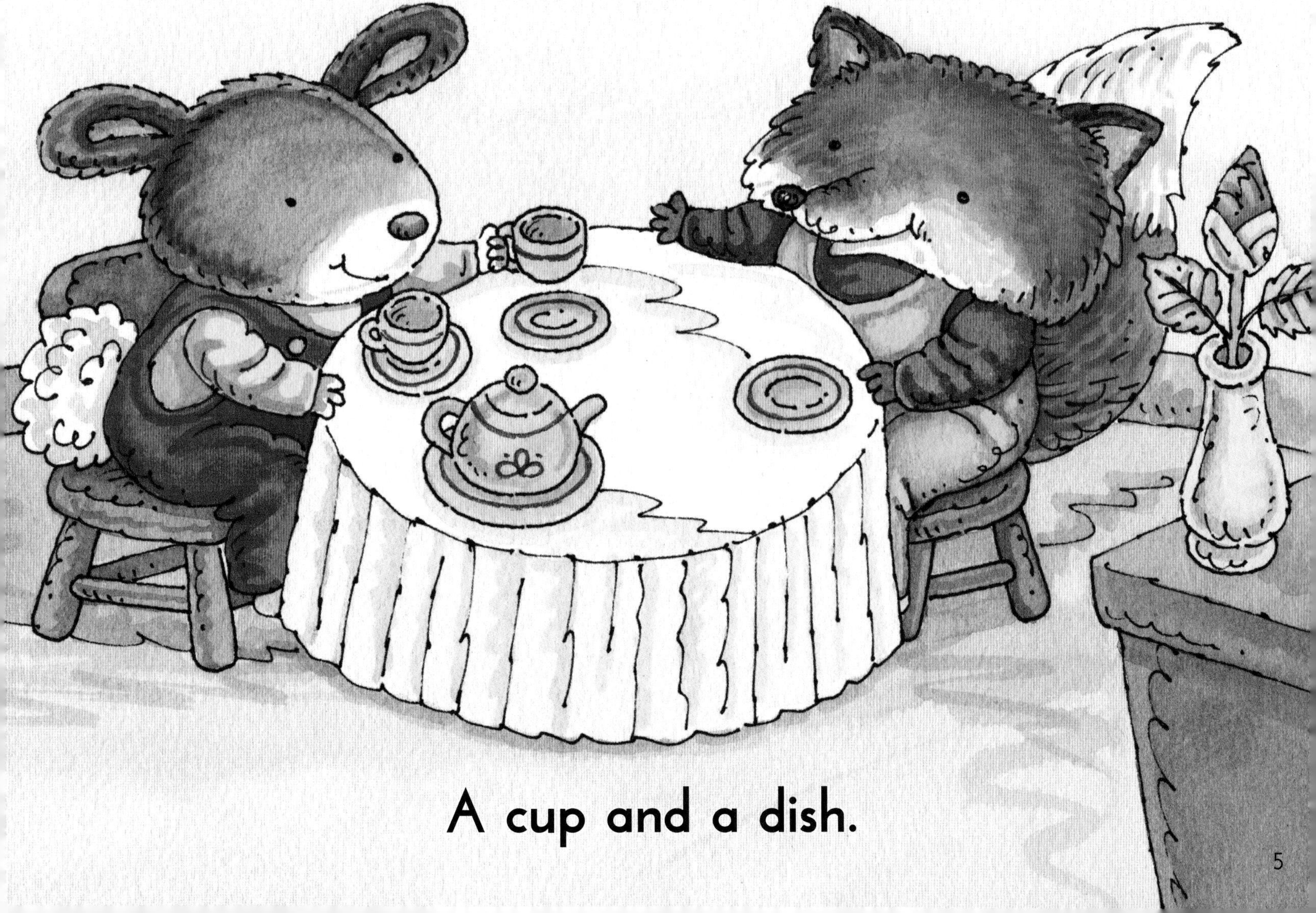

A cup and a dish.

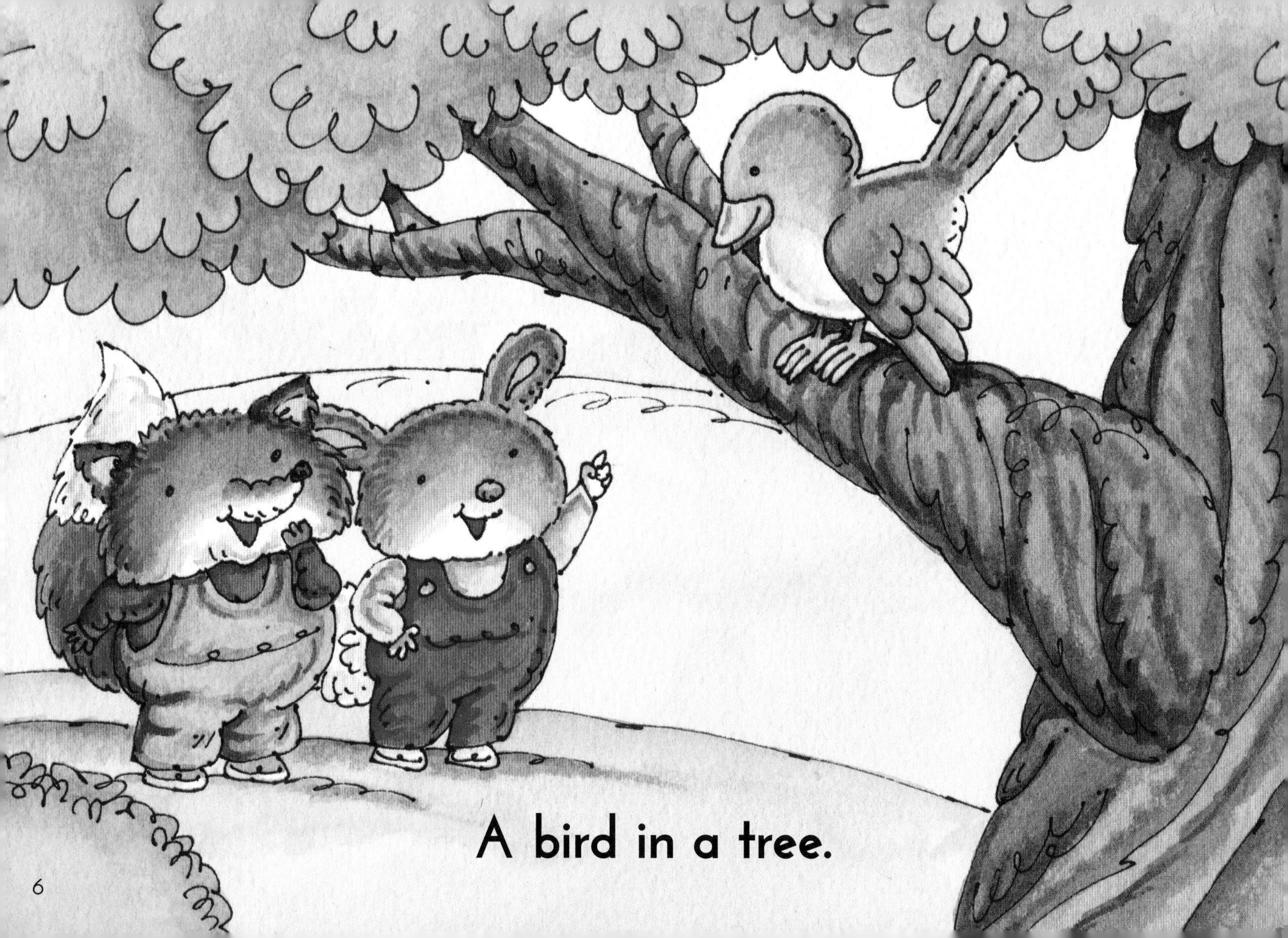

A bird in a tree.

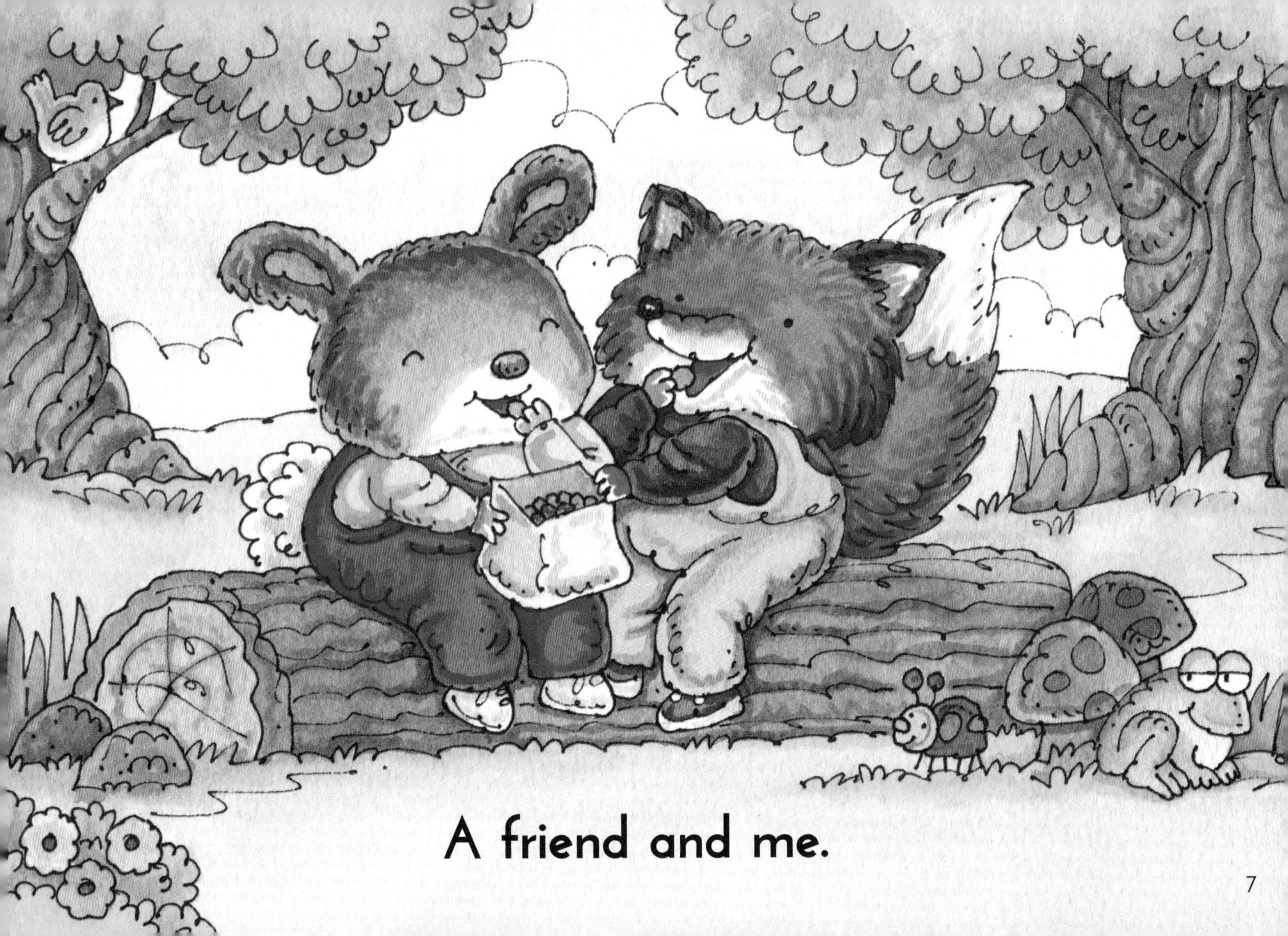

A friend and me.

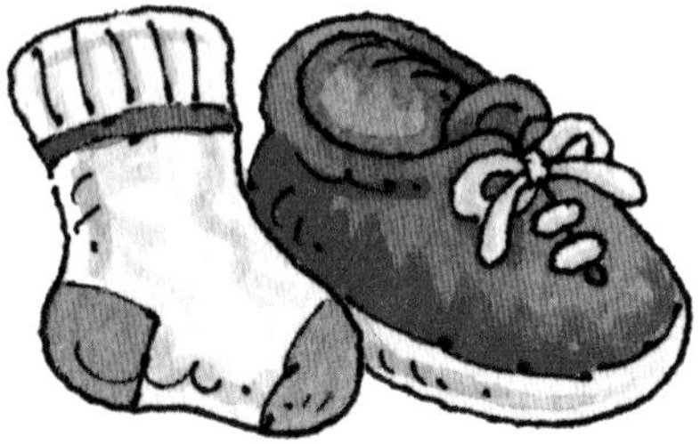

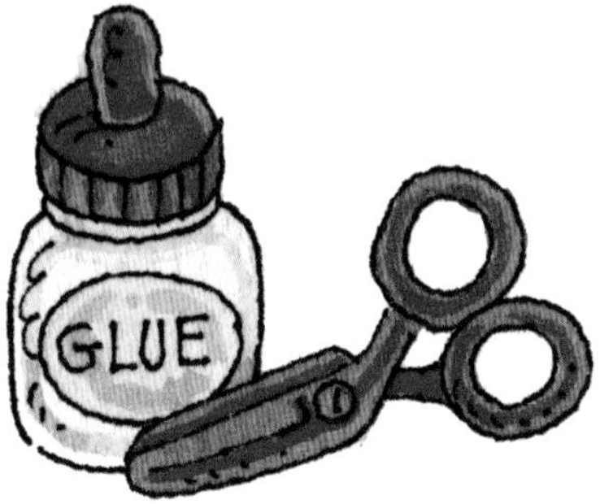

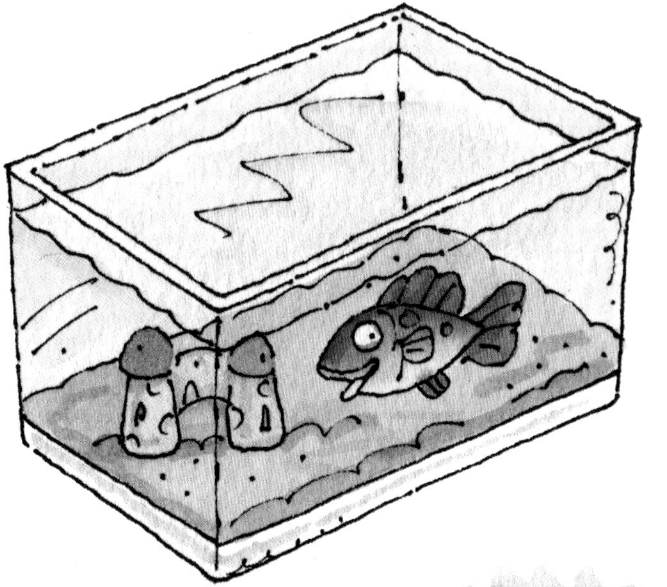

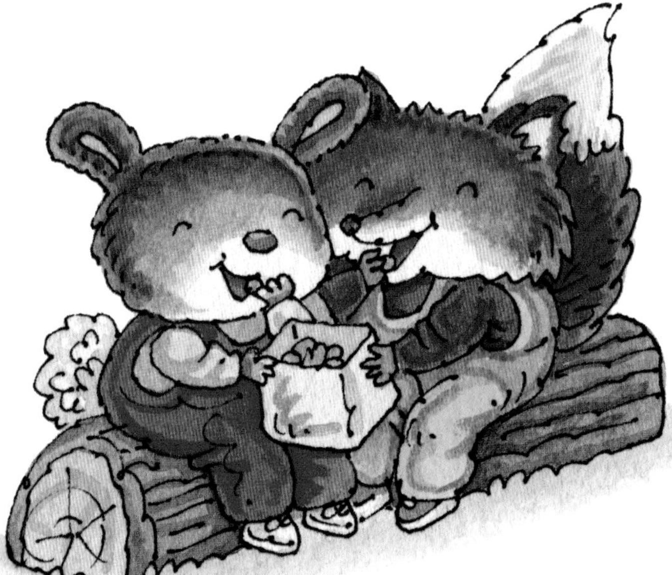

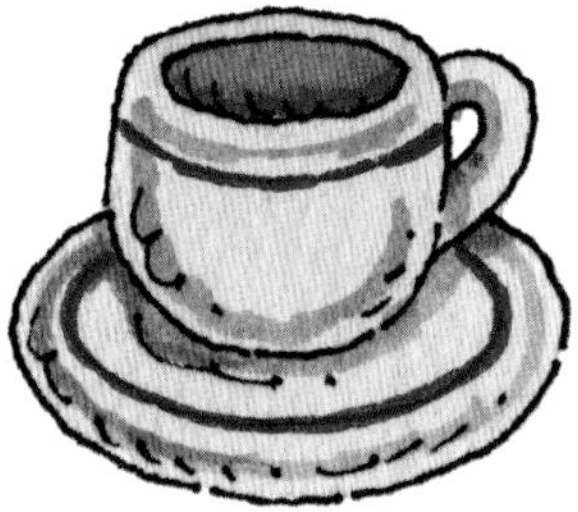

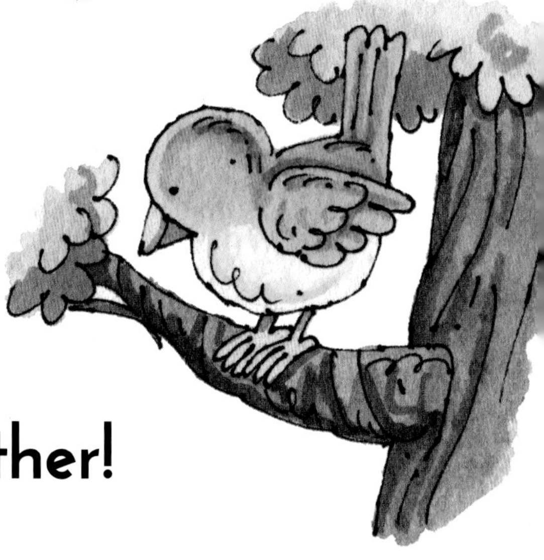

That's what goes together!